Guilt of a "W" terrorist

Guilt of a "W" terrorist

N-What!

iUniverse, Inc.
New York Lincoln Shanghai

Guilt of a "W" terrorist

iUniverse books may be ordered through booksellers or by contacting:

iUniverse
2021 Pine Lake Road, Suite 100
Lincoln, NE 68512
www.iuniverse.com
1-800-Authors (1-800-288-4677)

ISBN-13: 978-0-595-41874-9 (pbk)
ISBN-13: 978-0-595-86221-4 (ebk)
ISBN-10: 0-595-41874-0 (pbk)
ISBN-10: 0-595-86221-7 (ebk)

Printed in the United States of America

Contents

So I'm a writer?

I was 12, when I first witnessed a cold, thoughtless and bloody murder of a very special person in my life—my mother. My father returned home from work and an argument with my mother ensued about his HIV result. It was positive. Four months before that he caught her in bed with his best friend and their relationship had never been the same since then.

As they continued arguing, she reached in her purse on the kitchen table and drew out her gun on him. Shocked and enraged by this, he held her by the neck and grabbed a kitchen knife from the sink stabbing her repeatedly each time yelling, "I'm not dying alone bitch!"

My father killed my mother, he was sentenced to life in prison. After the death of my mother I was completely devastated and gave up with life. Going from foster home to foster home worsened everything so I ended up roaming the streets of Washington, DC.

Panhandling, sleeping at shelters, hot meals from different soup kitchens, breaking into cars was the order of my life.

The world is full of cold hearted people, not everybody though. I was rebuked and ignored, that is what most homeless people face. This humiliation made me give up completely on myself.

It was not long before one night a well-dressed young man walked up to me on his way to dreaming and loving at Dreams later renamed Love night club where I panhandled on Fridays and Saturdays. This man, Michael talked to me for almost two hours. We shared our stories, more so, telling me that no matter what happens in ones life, you can recollect yourself after a sorrowful situation. And for me to abandon myself the way I did was unacceptable, according to him.

A weekly meeting followed after that first encounter. We talked a lot, mostly about what I can do to change my living situation. He told me to write about him so I could earn some money and work on living a stable, somewhat comfortable life.

The following is a narrative about a *"w" terrorist* and a father proud of being a father—taking care of his business.

I didn't get much formal education, so my writing may get a lot of criticism and ridicule from literature experts and teachers of the English language. Matter of fact this publication may end up in the *Worst Published Books List*. I have utilized a mediocre style of writing-lousy sentence construction, punctuation, error in spelling and syntax, an incomplete, inappropriate and inconsistent flow of ideas. I doubt whether this publication will be a bestseller. Actually the bestseller of all time is the Bible, and I don't intend to break that record.

The text was supposed to be printed in a unique arch form—a style that helps ones muscles around the eyes and better retention of what is read, according to Michael. Okay, that is false. He wanted the text to be arched on each page to form a lowercase of the letter "M" when you open to read it. Yeah, "M" for Michael, you dig!

L-R
D-Baby, Ko-Ko and your father

A "w" terrorist

Respect of life and the dignity of the human person became passionate issues to him after he did something to become what he refers to as a "*w*" terrorist. He paid for an abortion. His woman had cheated on him and they mutually agreed to murder the unborn child. With so much anguish he almost pulled her back before she went in the doctor's murder room. Instead he tried to appease his conscience which was gnawing him deeply. Well, he figured he always gave her money without a care what she spent it on. And that application could be made then to justify the situation, he gave her $250 and she "spent" it on murdering an innocent, harmless unborn child at three months in her pregnancy. Only God knows what that unknown, unborn child would have grown up to be—may be a protégé with very outstanding talents, a doctor who would come up with a cure for some of the life threatening diseases that afflict humanity, may be the next political leader. Can you imagine murdering the next president, governor, senator, Pope or any other prominent person for that matter? That's outrageous. May be the unborn child would have been that person you were meant to be with but now you ended up with that disrespectful spouse, employer among other things No wonder there are numerous dysfunctional relations in the family, political upheavals, and many other social ills. In short, may be that unborn child would have saved the current and future disturbing situations. Again, that is according to Michael.

Daddy's ballers!

After the abortion, which did not help his relationship, he always questioned the morality of these two different, separate incidences; my father serving life in prison for killing my mother, and yet he has not been convicted for indirectly killing an innocent, harmless and unborn child. He had heard of cases where an individual is imprisoned for killing a pregnant woman and the charges include killing of the unborn child. He wondered why then wasn't he imprisoned for being an accomplice in the death of an unborn child?

His relentless quest for answers on life issues led him to found the Department of Bombland Security, a non-profit organization aimed at fundraising and disseminating information about culture of life activities worldwide.

When he called himself a *"w"* terrorist, "w" for womb, it was after following some of the terrible and deadly events happening around world. Living in a post September 11 world was complicated.

On the day when terrorists hijacked and flew planes in the Twin Towers he was in Amsterdam, Holland waiting for his flight to Washington, DC. All flights to the United States were cancelled and he made it to DC four days later. The scenes of the planes flying in World Trade Center kept being aired over and over at the airports' televisions. At first dismissed it as a preview of a newly released movie out of Hollywood until he grasped the seriousness of what had happened.

Anyway, after a terrorist attack, a lot is being reported about casualties, death, destruction of property, perpetrators of the attack and elevated security measures. According to Michael and his Department of Bombland Security, he tried to shed another perspective. Any terrorist attack harmed the unborn child. The real *war on terror* was started after Roe vs. Wade by the pro-life movement. He said Roe vs. Wade *legalized* womb terrorism against the unborn child and that in comparison, terrorists and the operations of supporters of abortion are similar.

Terrorist organizations and abortion groups have solid financial support for their activities. Terror cells and abortion clinics harm present and future civilizations. Sanger Margaret and Osama bin Laden may have a tight relationship. Again, these were Michael's thoughts as founder of Department of Bombland Security.

Daddy goin' bye-bye?

The guilt made him to cherish and appreciate life with his kids and the dignity of the human person. Abortion is a bomb to the womb.

This part is a semiautobiographical portrayal of Michael's visits to his children, D-Baby and Ko-Ko. His struggle with having a guilty conscience for being a *"w"* terrorist leading to an unconditional, undying love and care for his children as well respect of life.

D-Baby

Daddy's big boy, you will always be number one to your father!

The day was March 10th, 2002 when you were born. Your father had decided to move to Lima, Ohio. He made travel arrangements to fly to Columbus, Ohio from Washington, DC. The following day he arrived, and your grandmother Kim together with your Uncle Tad were at the airport to pick him up.

At the hospital, dainty and delicate, your father held you in his arms and fell in love with you! His number one big boy!

Chillin wit yo dad

Later that evening, he spent the night at your grandmother Kim's house on Virginia Lee Road where your great grandparents Art and Dot came to see you and then go down to Lima, Ohio with your father.

Life is what you make it baby, that was one of your father's favorites sayings. He had an unwavering faith in God regardless of his own sinful ways. He possessed a firm and sound education that one should always be ready to make lemonades from lemons that life will offer. HA! HA! That when all else fails, God's love and mercy will always prevail.

Unlike Washington, D.C Lima was laidback. His judgment upon arrival was that, Lima—*Lost In Middle America* was more family-oriented, but the racial divide was obvious. A good place to raise kids, and people had time to talk to each other! He found it rather amazing that people held lengthy conversations among each other. The hustle and bustle of D.C left little if any time at all to know somebody's last name.

Due to some legal challenges, he was not able to obtain any formal employment. He had gained an exceptional level of 'hood street sophistication just like Wall Street to survive anywhere on earth so long as he could communicate. The first time he was frustrated and self-conscious about speaking was when he once traveled to Belgium and could not communicate with any non-English speaking person! Alright back to Lima, he did numerous low-level jobs ranging from landscaping, plowing snow, remodeling housing units, baby sitting, all in order to take care of you. His mantra was, always look closely around you and see what you can do to improve yourself with what you have and are able to do right where you are. At four months old your mother visited Lima together with your grandmother Kim and Uncle Tad. Your mother and father started dating. Wow!

On February 3rd, 2003 your mother and father lost your "brother or sister" through a miscarriage. The incident was very traumatic and it tormented them for a long time especially your father. In March, your grandmother Kim hosted your first birthday party in her house. The celebration uplifted your father's hopes and dedication to always be there for you no matter what happened.

Later that summer, your mother and father moved in together in an apartment on Prospect Avenue which they made it as homely as possible. Around this time your mother informed your father that she was expecting another child. He was thrilled by the news. Deep within himself he knew he would be compelled to get a job earning more money than the meager sum he made from remodeling houses for a crafty landlord who doubled up as his employer.

A few months later, life became difficult due to reduced income and delayed pay by your father's landlord. Your mother's prenatal visits were becoming regular, fall was around the corner, food was getting low. Even one time the apartment unit where they stayed was without gas, electricity and water! Having no single item to prepare for the birth of your brother, in addition to all the other problems, your father had to do something sooner than later. He was always able to maintain a serene outlook on things even in the most trying situations. Armed with faith in God, he made a drastic decision—Leave Lima!

He had already settled and came to regard Lima as home. Now getting ready to leave "the Bean City" was heart wrenching. He called his long-time friend, Tom whom he had not talked to in about 10 months for help. They had traveled together extensively around the world. They promised each other to be there for one another through thick and thin. With that, Tom gladly welcomed your father back to the Washington, DC metropolitan area.

He packed mostly winter clothing and had asked you and your mother to move back to your grandmother Kim's on Prospect Ave. The departure to DC was very emotional, there were not so many people to bid farewell. He got on the Greyhound on the latter part of October 2003, and sobbed and slept and sobbed all the way to the nation's capital.

Upon arriving in DC, your father spent the next few days indoors because Tom was always at work. During these solitude times he read his Bible, prayed but slipped up when he started drinking Jack Daniel's whiskey from Tom's alcohol cabinet. That was the start of his excessive drinking habits. Sometimes out of desperation he would go across the street to Christ The King Catholic church and stay in the still and quiet presence of Our Lord Jesus. He converted to the Catholic faith when he was 18 and met the late Pope John Paul II two years later.

Roamin' in Rome, yo dad at the far left

He read quite a number of the late Pope's writings but never completed any. This was in part due to the depth of the writing which never gave an easy read and the length of each document. So he settled for more simplified, reduced and revised versions of the original documents. *Humane Vitae,* and *Theology of the Body* were some of his favorites.

In D.C. there was no time he did not think of you and your mother, who by now was about to give birth to your brother. On Thanksgiving Day he phoned your mother but did not succeed with that call.

He always had the ability to draw inner strength and be resilient in the face of adversity. This is when he made an ambitious effort to seek employment. Tom was generous to give him money for transportation to all places he needed to go. One thing that was always motivational was the thought of you, your mother and your *brother* yet to be born. With the same zeal and determination he had in Lima, he was positive that he would make it, that he already had the vision of being success-ful. All that was left was for him to manifest the dream by all means necessary.

He landed a job as a bathroom attendant at two night clubs working from Thursday through Sunday. The job was menial but he possessed a winning attitude that made the seven hours he had to put in pass like thirty minutes. The first night he took $500 in tips after subtracting what he had invested. At least now he would be able to get baby sup-plies for your *brother* yet to be born and Christmas gifts for you and mommy. Later in December he received a phone call from your mother and he was overjoyed to hear from her. They talked about different things; the clarity of your speech, you, being playful, and that seeing your father on her birthday would be the best gift. She told him that your *brother* was going to be born on February 19th, 2004—a day after his birthday!

With that, he sent her $300 for Christmas and they started talking on a regular basis. Alcohol had already become a problem for him. Once, your great grandmother Dot told him that sorrow and loneliness do *swim* through one's drunken state and resurface again resulting to added misery and depression.

When he was not working at the night clubs, he read books at the local library and went downtown DC in search of another job. His efforts paid off in mid—January 2004 when he was hired as a cashier for a sports store. By now he went ahead with a very rigorous schedule balancing two jobs hoping and praying that one day you, your *brother* and your mother will see each other again.

Ko-Ko

Only God loves you more than your father baby!

February 16th 2004, the day you were born, three days before your due date. What a great birthday gift for your father on his 26th birthday!

He *saw* you on the latter part of January the year you were born. He made a point to honor your mother's wish to visit Lima for her birthday. Upon arrival your mother and brother, D-Baby had the most jovial look on their faces to see your father again. Right there at the

Greyhound bus station after exchanging hugs and kisses he asked her to *see* you. He got down on one knee raised her stretched out T-shirt and *kissed* you and *rubbed* your big body self.

Hmmmmmmmmmmmmmmmmmm!

They had a lot of catching up to do. The day was spent at the malls, visiting your relatives. During these travels around Lima, your father and mother had a conversation about selecting your name. He wanted you to be his junior but she had other options. By the time they settled for *Kobe*, which by the way your father wanted it to be spelt *Kolbe*—they agreed that what really mattered was being good parents. He wanted to be more than a father,—he wanted to be a parent, see you grow, hear you mumble your first words, help you take your first steps, change your diapers; he wanted to be in your life, be there for you and your brother!

Like father like son

Lima still looked the same-abandoned buildings, stalled remodeling projects, litter on the streets was the usual sight on the south end, the north and west side of the city still maintained its unique look. Downtown was not any different, "sale" signs on store windows, a handful of cars on the parking lot, a few people on the sidewalks like always, these brought back nostalgic feelings to your father.

Your father marked you, fo' real!!

Dinner at Olive Garden that evening was where he proposed to your mother! Though still pregnant with you, they toast champagne to celebrate the occasion. Due to work obligations, he had to return to DC still working as a bathroom attendant and cashier.

Mid-morning on February 16th 2004, your father had a couple of work related matters to handle. Meanwhile, you *were* getting ready to *enter* this world! Returning home from his errands, your grand mother Kim had left messages for him to call her urgently. At 2:30PM, he heard your cry over the phone and was saddened by the fact that he was not there when you were born, something he always desired to witness. Your mother told him to go to the hospital's website and look at your photo which was going to be posted three days later. That was the *first* time he *saw* you! He even printed out the photo and stuck it on the wall above his bed and could not wait to hold you in his arms. Your birth was the best birthday blessing he had ever received and said that nothing would top that. In fact on D-Baby's birthday, March 10th he had a tattoo in Old English letters "D K" inked on his upper left arm.

Three is love

Later in April he came to Lima to see you! After taking a seventeen hour Grey Hound bus ride he was happy, overjoyed, thrilled, excited, there was no better description of how he felt when he saw you, he held you and he saw himself in you. He really marked you!

He held you most of the time during his visit, fixed your bottles though he preferred your mother to breast feed you, changed your diaper—the first time he did it he felt like he was going to break your tiny chubby legs.

Grow to be better than your father

Back in DC, he knew his love for you and your brother will always be present regardless of his distant presence in your lives. The knowledge of not being there to raise you almost haunted him daily, left him depressed and miserable. He sought solace in excessive consumption of alcohol and working longer hours. He knew he would have to rent a two bed-roomed apartment so that you, your mother and brother could come and stay with him in Washington, DC. This was a very difficult, expensive and time consuming task that became possible later in September.

Your father always made the daily monthly visits!

DeKo

DeKo, you were all smiles

D-Baby plus Ko-Ko equals DeKo. That's the joint name your father coined referring to you two.

Your father and mother talked mostly by phone. The long-distance relationship was very stressful. They were eager to see each other but because of the distance apart they tried to talk to each other phone as much as possible all with the aim of strengthening their love no matter how apart they were. The challenge with this was that your mother had to do it around your father's hectic schedule. All along your father would emphasize to her about the importance of his role in your upbringing—he wanted to be a father and a parent to you.

He could afford to come and see you each weekend. However, his schedule from two fulltime jobs made it impossible. He knew it would take a lot of time to plan his visits, and, he visited every month consistently. Once he made an emergency visit when Ko-Ko was hospitalized.

Y'all look dorky and goofy

In addition to his monthly visits, your father made a point to come to Lima for your birthdays and holidays—Memorial Day, Independence Day, Labor Day, Thanksgiving and Christmas.

He had you and your mother join him in DC after Thanksgiving of 2004. The fast paced lifestyle of the District intimidated your mother. This made your father to be very concerned. In spite of his grueling schedule, he spent as much time as he could with you and your mother. Still her loneliness persisted. He even risked losing his jobs by going late and leaving early to spend more time with her but this didn't do any good. He told her to maintain communication on a regular basis with the rest of the family, this did not help either. The situation was further complicated around Christmas time. He had booked three round trip plane tickets to Columbus, Ohio from Dulles international airport. Unfortunately, on the day of traveling the airport was very crowded that you all missed your flight.

Events that followed since then led to her decision to leave your father, saying she missed Lima and regretted moving to DC. On January 16th she flew with both of you to Columbus, Ohio where your grandmother received you and drove down to Lima.

This left your father very distressed. He could not fathom any part of that. He was under the impression that everything they did was mutual. The worse was the thought about all he did for you and your mother and that's the *thanks* he received! Little did he know that was the start of a painful and harsh reality of being alienated from you two.

More visits and more visits

In February he hosted a lavish birthday party dubbed "DeKo and Daddy Triple Fun" at your grand mother Kim's house. He cherished all the moments he spent with you but was always emotional when it was time to return to DC. Both of you would ask almost in unison, "daddy goin' bye-bye?"

Love, from mom and dad

Daddy goin' bye-bye?

Your father tried to have a cordial relationship with your mother for the sake of you. He knew that kids can sense the stress of a relationship between mother and father no matter how young they may be even when they cannot speak. In any case he knew they would have to keep in touch for any reason pertaining to your well being.

His favorite line was, *"where my boys at?"* whenever he called her to speak to you. D-Baby, you would talk without any direction, asked questions which did not have any relation to what the conversation was about. You talked about what you were doing—whether you were play-ing, eating cereal, watching cartoons. The funny part was when you always told him you were mimicking his laugh and at times you would put the phone down go about playing then get back on the phone and talk and talk. He always corrected your English. As "Daddy's big boy" you were to take lead as the big one. You always kept the phone to yourself and did not want to share with your brother unless your mother told you so…you were a *bad* butt!

D-Baby, don't mess with Ko-Ko!

Ko-Ko, you talked whenever you felt like though you loved hearing your father on the other end of the line. Then occasionally you would mumble something, giggle, and later hum a tune he always did when he fed you. As time went by you were able to say, "daddy" then you would do what your brother did, do your baby talk, put the phone down and just wanted to stay on the phone until your mother took it from you.

He always made a point to say "I love you babies, be good" before he hang up the phone with you. During his visits much of the time spent with you he expressed his love verbally, something which he felt was important for you to hear from a very early age. It was the same chorus—"Daddy goin bye—bye?" after talking to him on the phone. With that he always assured you that he was going to come to Lima.

As your father's pride and joy, he had a special "DeKo Goody" bag full of candy. He gave you candy whenever you were well behaved, something you never did!

Fun in the sun

When it came to buying gifts, he used to sign off *"Love, from dad"*. He changed that because he did not want you growing up comparing what your mother buys for you against what he bought for you. Even when it was obvious he bought anything he still told you that mommy and daddy did shopping together for you. And that is when he starting signing off,

Love,
from mother and father

Father's Day ain't shit

Your father said that the best days in somebody's life are when one is born and the day one dies. Between the two, one's birthday is the best. Weird as it may sound that was his thinking. Out of all celebrations one can have in a lifetime, the priority of festivities should never out do Christmas, Easter and one's birthday.

DeKo, get yo clown on!

According to him there was nothing special about Valentine's Day, Mother's Day, Father's Day or any day given significance over something that can and should be done all year round. Still he did something unique for your mother around any of these days. As a father, he said that all days in any given year are Father's Days. He knew and felt that fatherhood is a task to be done daily.

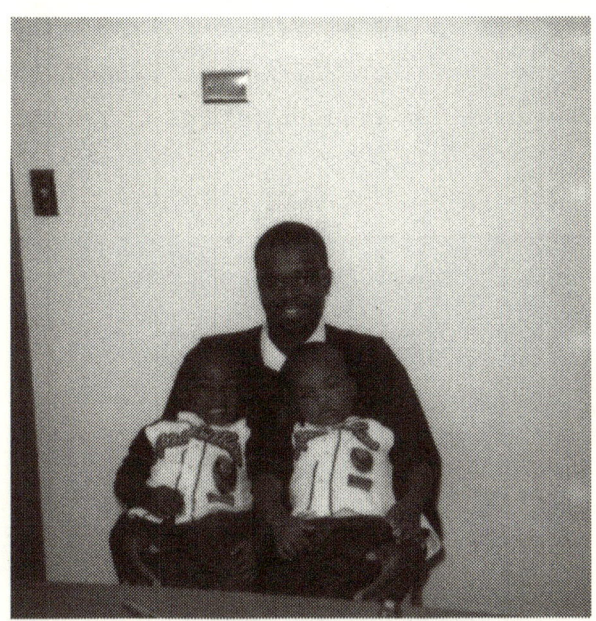

DeKo, a father's Most Valuable Babies!!

Your mother had him pay child support for Ko-Ko, something he was very upset about. He did not see any reason why he should pay child support. You were his M V B's—Most Valuable Babies, and that is how he treated you. He expressed his sentiments to me concerning this matter;

"I'm not an irresponsible man. I take care of my kids and provide for them by all means available. This child support shit is crazy! I ain't the type of nigga that needs to be forced to take care of his kids. I clothe 'em, feed 'em, hang out with them and the whole nine. I make sure they eat right though all they want is McNasties, candy and other junk shit True there be cases of them deadbeat assholes who neglect their responsibility yet keep having babies all over the map. Dumb ass niggas like that need to be forced to take care of they kids. See, I'm a smart mo'fucka! I love my boys dearly, I take a bullet for them, you feel me? On the flip side of this shit, you see some

broads don't wanna get a 9 to 5 instead makin' a livin' off they own babies. Ain't that some sad, sorry shit? DeKo my most valuable babies and them support mo'fuckas are fuckin' up by puttin' a dollar amount I gotta pay for mine.

He said, "Father's Day ain't shit"

Fuck all that support enforcement shit, why somebody gotta tell me how much to pay? And that bullshit of how often I can see him? Don't get me wrong some dumb ass niggas deserve that shit, not me and that's fo' real. Child support or no child support I take care of mine, fuck this."

Web warrior, dot com hustler,
dot com warrior,

Alright, who's gonna play football?

To prepare for your future, your father did almost anything he could possibly do other than formal employment. Armed with muscular belief in self reliance, he taught himself basic computer skills and went ahead to utilize the world of the internet. He considered himself a *webber, web warrior, dot com hustler, dot com warrior,* titles he formulated as his occupation.

Funny faces!

Having come to terms about how atrocious his role was in the murder of an innocent, unborn child he started michaelochieng2@yahoo.com, the world's first worst and expensive email catalogue trade order to fundraise for pro-life and pro-family causes and stop womb terrorism.

Even though he was, a womb terrorist, meeting your father helped me respect life and the dignity of the human person, core values he hopes you will uphold. These turn helped me start living again since the death of my mother and life imprisonment of my father.

Life is what you make it to be

978-0-595-41874-9
0-595-41874-0

www.ingramcontent.com/pod-product-compliance
Lightning Source LLC
Chambersburg PA
CBHW050344290526
45785CB00006B/2625